THIS BOOK BELONGS TO

____

____

____

ISBN: 9798573105581
Imprint: Independently published

PRANAB PUBLISHING

ALL RIGHTS RESERVED BY PRANAB MAHATA

COLORING BOOK FOR ADULTS (MANDALAS)

www.ingramcontent.com/pod-product-compliance
Lightning Source LLC
Chambersburg PA
CBHW081619250726
48657CB00009B/2622